Activities

Quick Tests

Alison Head and Louis Fidge

Speaking and listening (1)

Interviewing someone is a great way to see if you can listen
carefully and remember what was said – it's fun, too!

1 Interview a relative who is older than you about what it was like when they
went to school. Plan some questions to ask them, using the words in the box to
help you.

a ____

b ____

c ____

d ____

e ____

lunchtime

games

assembly

homework

lessons

PE

teachers

uniform

2 Can you remember what they said? Write an account of what you remember
below. Was their school very similar or different to your experiences?

____

____

____

____

____

____

____

____

____

____

____

Homophones

Homophones are words that **sound the same**, but have **different meanings** or **spellings**.

You need to think about the whole sentence to know which is the right word to use.

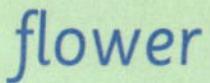

flour   flower

We bought some **flour** to bake the cake.

I picked a red **flower**.

1 **Write homophones for these words.**

a knew _______________

b hole _______________

c grate _______________

d there _______________

e two _______________

f herd _______________

g sea _______________

h be _______________

i for _______________

j write _______________

2 **Write a sentence for each word to show you know how to use it correctly.**

a plaice _We had plaice and chips.___________________

b place _I know the place you mean.__________________

c threw _______________________________________

d through _______________________________________

e son _______________________________________

f sun _______________________________________

g floor _______________________________________

h flaw _______________________________________

i main _______________________________________

j mane _______________________________________

Verb endings

Verbs tell us what a person or thing is **doing**. The ending of the verb changes depending on **who** is doing the activity and whether it has already happened (past), is happening now (present) or will happen (future).

she walk**ed**   she walk**s**   she will be walk**ing**

Sometimes the spelling of the verb changes when the ending is added.

1 Complete the rows by adding the correct ending to each verb.

	s	ed	ing
a jump	jumps	jumped	____________
b prefer	prefers	____________	preferring
c kick	____________	kicked	kicking
d grab	grabs	____________	grabbing
e garden	gardens	gardened	____________
f save	saves	____________	____________
g lift	____________	lifted	____________

2 Rewrite these sentences, using the correct form of the verb in bold.

a The car **stops** a few seconds ago at the traffic lights.

____

b Yesterday Dad **limit** the number of chips he ate.

____

c I **carrying** the shopping home for Gran yesterday.

____

d Mum always **washing** the car on Saturdays after we go swimming.

____

e It **beginning** to rain last night.

____

f Jenny always **exploring** the rock pools as soon as she gets to the beach.

____

Suffixes *ship*, *ness* and *ment*

We can add suffixes to the **ends** of some words to change their meaning.

Ship, *ness* and *ment* are suffixes which do not change the spelling of the root word.

sponsor + **ship** = sponsorship

fair + **ness** = fairness

battle + **ment** = battlement

The only exception is if the word ends in a consonant followed by *y*, when you change the *y* to *i* before adding the suffix.

tidy + **ness** = tidiness

1 Complete these word sums.

a merry + ment = _______________

b kind + ness = _______________

c fit + ness = _______________

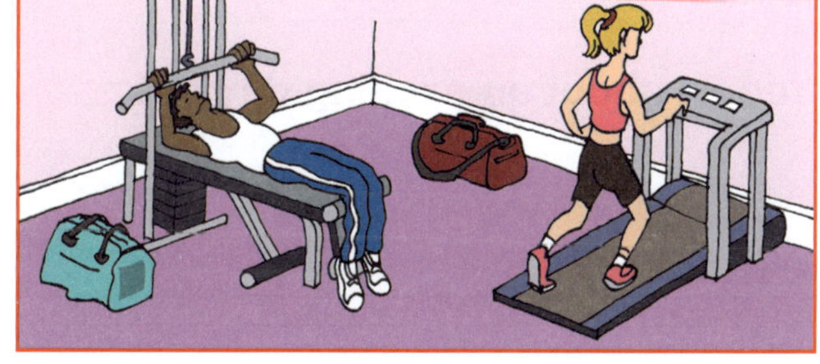

d enjoy + ment = _______________

e lazy + ness = _______________

f member + ship = _______________

g silly + ness = _______________

h friend + ship = _______________

i careless + ness = _______________

j happy + ness = _______________

2 Choose *ship*, *ness* or *ment* to add to each of these words. Then write down the new word.

a measure _______________

b tidy _______________

c nasty _______________

d employ _______________

e state _______________

f wicked _______________

g fellow _______________

h apprentice _______________

i replace _______________

j champion _______________

Speaking and listening (2)

Giving spoken or oral reports is a great way to practise speaking clearly and confidently. Spoken reviews are another good way to make sure you can organise ideas, and report them orally.

1 Give a spoken review of your favourite film to a grown-up.

a What is the title of your favourite film?

____

b Who is your favourite character, and why?

____

c What, in your opinion, is the most exciting thing that happens in the film?

____

d How do you feel about the ending? Does it resolve any problems that arose during the story?

____

2 Make notes to help you plan a spoken report about an exciting day out.

a Where did you go, and why?

____

b What transport did you use to get there? Was it far? How long did it take?

____

c Describe what happened during the day.

____

d Would you want to go again if you got the chance? Give reasons for your answer.

____

e Would you recommend the day out to a friend?

____

Alphabetical order

Putting words in alphabetical order helps us to find information in **dictionaries** and **indexes**.

If the first two letters of a group of words are the same, we can use the third and fourth letters to put the words in alphabetical order.

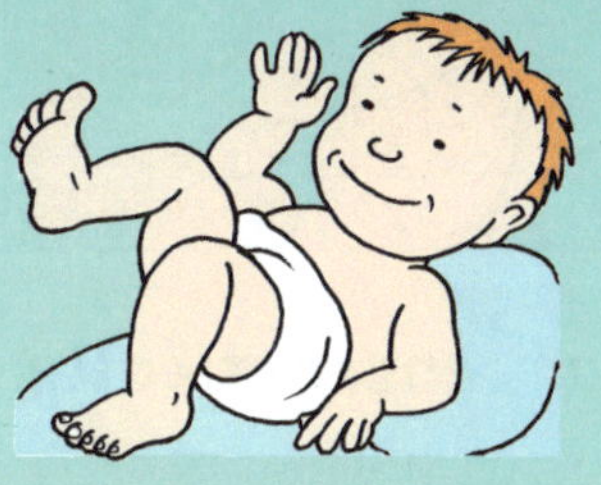

ba**b**y

ba**g**gage

ba**l**l

a **b** c d e f **g** h i j k **l** m n o p q r s t u v w x y z

check you know your alphabet.

1 Use the third bold letter to find each word in the box. Then write the missing letters so the words are in alphabetical order. The first one has been done for you.

sunny   super   suspect   submarine   sudden

summer   sugar   suitable   success

a su**b**marine

b su**c**______

c su**d**______

d su**g**______

e su**i**______

f su**m**______

g su**n**______

h su**p**______

i su**s**______

2 Write these words in alphabetical order, using the third and fourth letters.

hair   hare   hat   hail
harp   hard   haste   have

a ______

b ______

c ______

d ______

e ______

f ______

g ______

h ______

Adverbs

Adverbs tell us **how** a person or thing does something.

I walked **quickly** to school.

The fish swam **energetically**.

e.g. Angrily, my sister stormed from the room.

1 Complete the word sums to spell these adverbs correctly.

a complete + ly = _______________________

b comic + ly = _______________________

c usual + ly = _______________________

d sleepy + ly = _______________________

e bad + ly = _______________________

f total + ly = _______________________

g humble + ly = _______________________

h basic + ly = _______________________

i gentle + ly = _______________________

2 Think of a suitable adverb to complete these sentences. Write your adverb.

a The mouse scurried _______________________ away.

b My sister stormed _______________________ from the room.

c Gemma thought _______________________ about the maths problem.

d The star shone _______________________ in the sky.

e Liam dawdled _______________________ home.

f Jess _______________________ scribbled down the phone number.

g My naughty brother behaved _______________________.

h Dad patted the dog _______________________.

i We talked _______________________ in the library.

3. Now write some interesting sentences starting with an adverb.

Making verbs

We can turn some nouns and adjectives into verbs by adding **suffixes** like *ate, en, ify* or *ise*.

With most words you can just add the suffix. If the word already has a suffix, or ends in *e* or *y*, the suffix or final letter must usually be removed before you add the new suffix.

1 Complete these word sums to make new verbs.

a deep + en = ___________________

b short + en = ___________________

c standard + ise = ___________________

d apology + ise = ___________________

e note + ify = ___________________

f elastic + ate = ___________________

g pure + ify = ___________________

h formal + ise = ___________________

i wake + en = ___________________

j medic + ate = ___________________

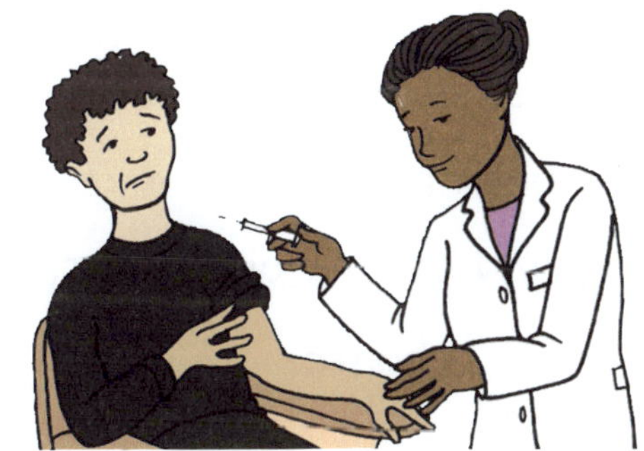

2 Add *ate, en, ify* or *ise* to these words to make verbs.

a intense ___________________

b real ___________________

c strength ___________________

d simple ___________________

e hard ___________________

f glory ___________________

g haste ___________________

h class ___________________

i serial ___________________

j weak ___________________

Choose 6 verbs & use each to write a sentence.

Irregular verbs

When verbs are used to tell us what a person or thing has already done, most end in *ed*. This is called the past tense.

Present
I **look** at the book.

Past
Yesterday I look**ed** at the book.

Some verbs have their own spelling patterns, especially in the past tense. These are known as irregular verbs.

I **keep** rabbits.   I **kept** rabbits.

1 **These past tense verbs are wrongly spelt. Write them correctly.**

a I hurted my hand.

b Sam putted his toys away.

c Claire runned home.

d Mum bringed my tea.

e I sended you a letter.

f The autumn leaves falled from the trees.

2 **Rewrite these sentences, starting with the words in bold. Make sure you spell the past tense verbs correctly. The first one has been done for you.**

a I eat my birthday cake.

Yesterday, *I ate my birthday cake.*

b Jamilla buys a comic.

Last week, _______________________

c Ali draws a picture.

Earlier today, _______________________

d I am tired.

Last night, _______________________

e I can swim.

When I was four, _______________________

f I tell you a secret.

Yesterday, _______________________

Now choose 3 sentence starters and write 3 sentences of your own.

Commas

Commas show us when to **pause** in a sentence.

They are also useful for **breaking up** longer sentences.

Which is your coat, Alex?

Jo, my friend, is eight years old.

1 **Add the missing commas to these sentences.**

a After tea we played football.

b Find your trainers Paul.

c Suddenly the lights went out.

d Judy and James from next door came shopping with us.

e My hat which is black matches my scarf.

f Last Tuesday after school I went skating.

2 **Rewrite these sentences, putting the commas in the correct place.**

a Tomorrow we, are playing football.

____

b The ink which, was blue stained, the carpet.

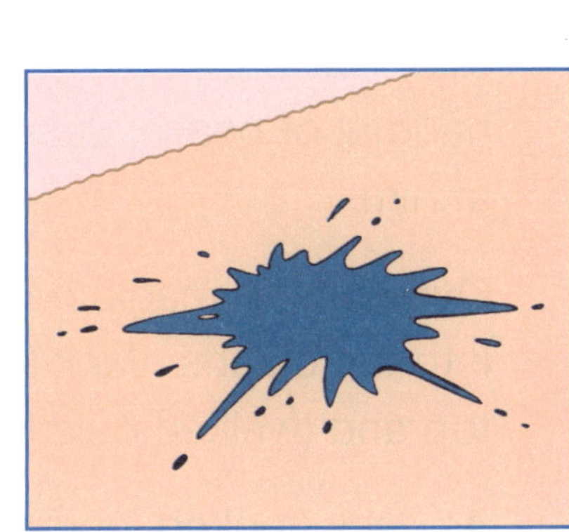

____

c Eventually Jane, won the game.

____

d It's, time to go Ali.

____

e While we were on, holiday we stayed in a hotel.

____

f At, school in my classroom is a display about, trains.

____

Powerful verbs

Verbs tell us what a person or thing
is **doing**.

*The dog **runs**.*

Powerful verbs also tell us **how** a person
or thing does something. Sometimes they
tell us so much, we do not need adverbs.

1 Sort each verb in the box into its correct group. Then add one more
suitable verb of your own to each group.

> hobbles   argues   devours   munches   shuffles   dictates   chews   declares   ambles

walks	says	eats
a ________________	b ________________	c ________________
________________	________________	________________
________________	________________	________________
________________	________________	________________

2 Read the fairytale. Then choose a powerful verb from the box to
use instead of the verbs and adverbs in brackets.

Jack and his mother were very poor. One day, Jack's mother (sternly
told) ________________ him to sell their cow. When he sold it for a
handful of beans, Jack's mother (shouted loudly) ________________
at him.

Overnight, a magic beanstalk (grew rapidly) ________________ up
into the clouds. Jack (climbed quickly) ________________ to the
top and (walked quietly) ________________ past the sleeping giant.

As Jack (looked longingly) ________________ at some bags of
gold, the giant woke up, so he (quickly collected) ________________
the gold and (ran away) ________________ down the beanstalk.

When he reached the bottom, Jack's mother (cut quickly)
________________ away at the beanstalk. The giant (fell heavily)
________________ to the ground, and Jack and his mother lived
happily ever after.

> grabbed
>
> shot
>
> ordered
>
> crashed
>
> yelled
>
> clambered
>
> fled
>
> hacked
>
> gazed
>
> crept

Fronted adverbials

An adverbial is a word or phrase used like an adverb. Adverbs –
and adverbials – add information or details to verbs. Adverbials
explain **where**, **how** or **when** something happens.

He ate his dinner **after the sun went down.**

verb   adverbial

Fronted adverbials are words and phrases at the
beginning of a sentence, used to describe the action
that follows. Fronted adverbials are usually followed by a comma.

After the sun went down, he ate his dinner.

fronted adverbial

1 **Draw a line to match each fronted adverbial to the most sensible
sentence ending.**

a	Before the sun rose,	he watched the stars.
b	In front of the baker's	I'll make lots of festive cakes and biscuits.
c	All night long,	he packed his bags.
d	Before Christmas,	he waited for his lunch.
e	Under a blanket of leaves,	she watched out of the window.
f	As quickly as he could,	the hedgehog slept.
g	All day,	she ate her breakfast.

2 **Write a fronted adverbial for these sentence endings. Don't forget to put a
comma after the fronted adverbial!**

a ____ she watched television.

b ____ he waited for his friends.

c ____ the cat meowed.

d ____ the woman giggled.

e ____ the man climbed.

f ____ they wondered.

g ____ she walked away.

Expressing time, place and cause

We can express time, place and cause in a sentence using conjunctions, adverbs and prepositions.

Conjunction

I went home **after** school.

Adverb

Soon, I shall go on holiday!

Preposition

I fell asleep **during** the afternoon.

1 **Underline the preposition, adverb or conjunction that expresses time.**

a Can you hold this while I eat please?

b I went to the shops before work.

c I went to the park after school.

d It will be home time soon, children.

e I ate popcorn during the film.

2 **Write a sentence using each of these words.**

a therefore ____

b when ____

c before ____

d soon ____

e during ____

f because ____

g after ____

Tricky plurals

Plural means **more than one** of something.

When you spell plurals, there are rules you have to follow.

Words ending in *f* usually change to *ves* in the plural.

Words ending *ff* just add *s*.

leaf

lea**ves**

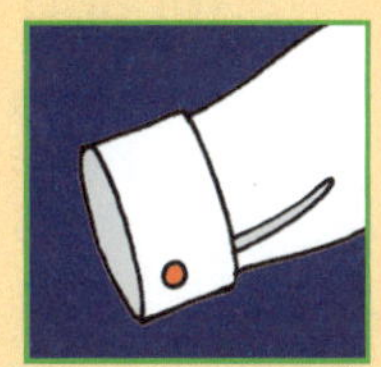

cu**ff**

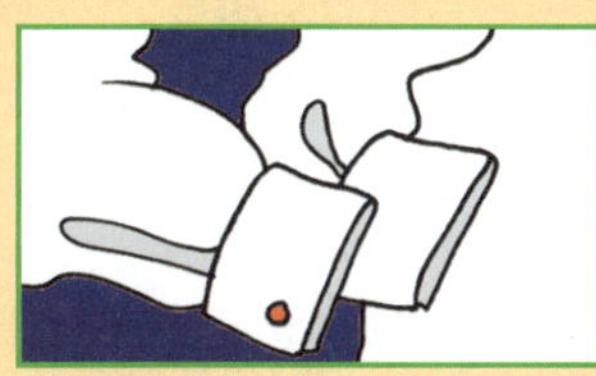

cu**ffs**

1 Underline the correct plural spelling for each word.

a **sniff**   snives   snifs   sniffs

b **half**   halves   halfs   halffs

c **puff**   puves   pufs   puffs

d **cliff**   clifs   clives   cliffs

e **scarf**   scarves   scarfs   scuves

f **scuff**   scufs   scuffs   scuves

g **calf**   calves   calfs   calffs

h **thief**   thiefs   thieves   thiefes

i **yourself**   yourselfs   yourselves   yourselff

j **knife**   knifes   kniffes   knives

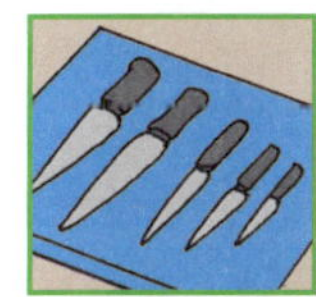

2 Write the plural form of these words.

a loaf   _________________

b self   _________________

c sheriff   _________________

d cuff   _________________

e wolf   _________________

f wife   _________________

g bluff   _________________

h shelf   _________________

i elf   _________________

j scoff   _________________

Choosing words

Choosing the right words for your writing is important.

Some words don't tell us very much.

*We had a **good** time at the party.*

Other words are more powerful and tell us much more.

*We had a **fantastic** time at the party.*

1 Draw a line to match each word with a more interesting alternative. The first one has been done for you.

a	hungry		hilarious
b	tired		terrifying
c	nice		parched
d	nasty		horrible
e	scary		starving
f	dry		lovely
g	wet		exhausted
h	funny		drenched

2 Rewrite these sentences, choosing a better word to replace the words in bold.

a It is **hot** today.

____

b We **got** some crisps at the shop.

____

c Kate **made** some biscuits.

____

d The mouse was **small**.

____

e We had lunch and **then** we went to the cinema.

____

Expanded noun phrases

Expanded noun phrases add **interest** to your writing by giving more **information** and **descriptions**. Expansion can happen both before and after the noun.

The monster roared. ➡️ The **scaly** monster, **with long dripping fangs**, roared.

1 Rewrite these sentences to make them more exciting by using expanded noun phrases.

a The cat jumped.

____

b The wind blew.

____

c A rabbit hopped up the lane.

____

d My mum laughed.

____

2 Write a sentence about each of these nouns. Use expanded noun phrases to make things exciting for your reader.

a bat _______________________________________

b kitten _____________________________________

c ghost ______________________________________

d woman _____________________________________

e fairy ______________________________________

f ship _______________________________________

g badger _____________________________________

Making adjectives

Adjectives **describe** things or people. We can often make adjectives by adding a suffix to a noun or verb.

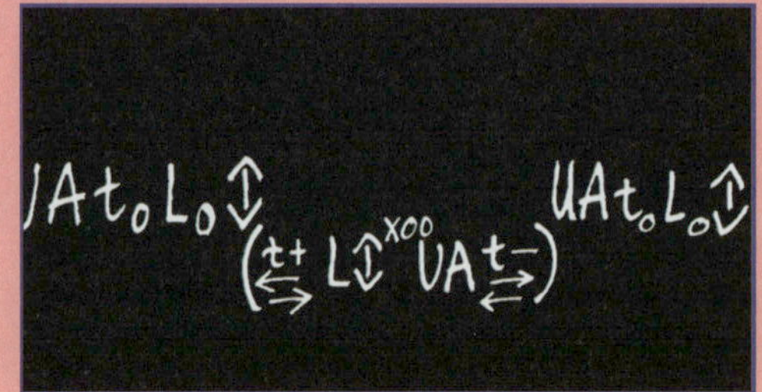

bore + ing = bor**ing**

Words ending in a single *e* drop the *e* when adding *ing* or *able.*

beauty + ful = beauti**ful**

Words ending in *y* change the *y* to *i* when adding *ful* or *able.*

1 Complete these word sums to turn these nouns and verbs into adjectives.

a shock + ing = _______________

b wash + able = _______________

c trust + worthy = _______________

d beauty + ful = _______________

e rely + able = _______________

f acid + ic = _______________

g road + worthy = _______________

h amuse + ing = _______________

i break + able = _______________

j pain + ful = _______________

2 Choose *ful* or *able* to make adjectives. Then write the new words.

a wish + _______ = _______________

b agree + _______ = _______________

c envy + _______ = _______________

d hope + _______ = _______________

e wonder + _______ = _______________

f care + _______ = _______________

g adore + _______ = _______________

h help + _______ = _______________

i value + _______ = _______________

j mercy + _______ = _______________

Choose 6 adjectives & write 6 interesting sentences.

More adjectives

Adjectives can help us to compare things or people.

Comparative adjectives compare two things – *bigger, smaller*.

Kate's cat is **bigger** than mine.

Superlative adjectives describe the limit of a quality – *biggest, smallest, most enormous*.

But Mina's cat is the **biggest** of all.

1 Decide whether the adjective in each sentence is comparative or superlative. Then tick the correct box.

	comparative	superlative
a This winter is the coldest on record.	☐	☐
b I live closer to the school than you do.	☐	☐
c I chose the least difficult question.	☐	☐
d My sister is younger than me.	☐	☐
e We saw the longest snake at the zoo.	☐	☐
f Diamonds are more valuable than pearls.	☐	☐
g My house is bigger than yours.	☐	☐
h The theme park was the most exciting place I've ever been.	☐	☐

2 Complete the rows with comparative and superlative adjectives.

	comparative adjectives	superlative adjectives
a	taller	__________
b	__________	narrowest
c	more amazing	__________
d	__________	best
e	older	__________
f	__________	most delicious
g	stranger	__________
h	__________	least interesting

Apostrophes for contraction

If two words are used together a lot, we can sometimes join them together. We do this by taking out some of the letters and putting an apostrophe in their place.

do not → don't

I am → I'm

1 **Circle the incorrect contractions.**

a **It's Its'** my birthday tomorrow.

b Jake is off school today because **hes he's** ill.

c I **didn't did'nt** do my homework.

d Unless we hurry **wel'l we'll** miss the bus.

e Dad **wo'nt won't** be home until later.

f My brother **wouldn't would'nt** let me watch TV.

g **You're Your're** my best friend.

h **Theyve They've** forgotten their bags.

2 **Rewrite these sentences, replacing the bold words with a contraction.**

a We **must not** speak in class.

____

b You can play football after **you have** done your homework.

____

c He **should not** have eaten so much cake.

____

d I **cannot** ice skate very well.

____

e They **could not** find our house.

____

More apostrophes

Possessive apostrophes are used to tell us when something **belongs** to somebody or something.

With single or collective nouns, the apostrophe usually goes before the *s*.

With plurals ending in *s*, the apostrophe usually goes after the *s*.

The people**'s** shoes

The man**'s** hat

The girl**s'** bags

1 Write the missing apostrophes in these phrases.

a the womans bag

b the boys heads

c the childs toy

d the peoples books

e two dogs baskets

f the suns rays

g three footballers boots

h a cats tail

2 Write down the shortened form of each phrase. The first one has been done for you.

a the wings of a bird   *a bird's wings*

b the pens belonging to the boys

c the cat belonging to Kim

d the parcels belonging to Sam

e the car belonging to my parents

f the rattles belonging to the babies

g the wallet belonging to my dad

h the sweets belonging to the children

More suffixes

Sometimes you can add two suffixes to the end of a word.

hope + **ful** + **ly** = hopefully

Sometimes you can add more than one different suffix to a word.

relate + **ion** = relation

relate + **ive** = relative

1 Complete these word sums. Remember the spelling rules for adding suffixes.

a grate + full + ly = _______________________

b converse + ation + ally = _______________________

c energy + etic + ally = _______________________

d photograph + ic + ally = _______________________

e thank + full + ly = _______________________

f joy + full + ly = _______________________

g horrify + ic + ally = _______________________

h respect + full + ly = _______________________

2 Pick two different suffixes from the box that can be added to each of these words. The first one has been done for you.

a correct   correct _ion_______   correct _ly_______

b product   product_______   product_______

c construct   construct_______   construct_______

d extreme   extreme_______   extreme_______

e act   act_______   act_______

f real   real_______   real_______

g oppress   oppress_______   oppress_______

h miss   miss_______   miss_______

ive

ly

ion

ist

Rhyming patterns

Poets use rhyme in different ways.

Some poems have **alternate rhyming lines**.

Snow *falls*,
Wind *blows*,
Bird *calls*,
Hungry *crows*.

Some lines rhyme in pairs. These are called **rhyming couplets**.

Sunny *days*,
Warm *rays*,
Burning *down*,
Grass *brown*.

Some poems use **no rhyme** at all.

Rain *splashes*,
Wet *feet*,
Dripping *trees*,
Black *puddles*.

1 Write whether each poem has alternate rhyming lines, rhyming couplets or no rhyme.

a

This poem has

____

____

b

This poem has

____

____

c

This poem has

____

____

2 Add two lines to each of these poems, making sure you match the rhyming patterns.

a Packed bags,
Luggage tags,
Clutching passport,
Crowded airport,

____

____

b Christmas tree,
Gifts below,
Treats for me,
There on show,

____

____

Making notes

When we make notes, we only need to write down the **key words**.

1 **Underline the key words in each sentence.**

a Molly and Sam are coming to tea.

b I have gone for lunch, but I will be back at noon.

c My birthday is in December.

d Remember you are playing football on Saturday.

e I have Maths and English homework to do.

f We need to buy some milk and bread.

2 **Write a full sentence for each set of notes.**

a Tea in oven.

____

b Brownies, Town Hall, 6pm.

____

c Lucy's party, Friday, buy gift.

____

d In garden, come round back.

____

e Mum rang. Running late.

____

f Car fixed. Please collect.

____

Prefixes

Prefixes are letter strings added to the beginning of root words to **change** their **meaning**. Here are some examples of prefixes and their meanings.

re back, again	***super*** above
sub under	***anti*** against
inter between, among	***auto*** self, own

1 Use the prefixes to help you write the meanings of these words. If you do not know the words, look them up in the dictionary.

a international ___________________________

b remake ___________________________

c automobile ___________________________

d submarine ___________________________

e antidote ___________________________

f replay ___________________________

g superior ___________________________

2 Draw a line to match each prefix to its correct ending.

a re   standard

b sub   place

c inter   biotics

d re   val

e anti   vise

f super   veal

g auto   mobile

Nouns and pronouns

Pronouns help to make writing flow more easily. If you used nouns all of the time, you just repeat yourself.

The dog walked into the garden. The dog jumped up at the fence and barked, and then the dog lapped up some water.

*The dog walked into the garden. **She** jumped up at the fence and barked, and then **she** lapped up some water.*

1 Change the repeated nouns to pronouns. Rewrite the sentences.

a The cat likes milk. The cat drinks it regularly.

____

b Birds fly into our garden. The birds like our pond.

____

c A man walked along the beach. The man picked up shells.

____

d The women were running. The women were keeping fit.

____

2 Write five sentences using a noun and a pronoun each time.

a ____

b ____

c ____

d ____

e ____

Punctuating speech

When using inverted commas (or speech marks), we have to follow some rules about punctuation and capital letters.

Sometimes we write who is speaking before we write what they say.

Attia said, "Let's go and play!"

Put a comma before the inverted commas. The full stop, question mark or exclamation mark at the end of the sentence goes inside the inverted commas.

Sometimes we write what they say first, then write who is speaking.

"Great, let's go," said Mari.

The first word of a piece of speech always starts with a capital letter.

A comma, question mark or exclamation mark at the end of the speech is used inside the inverted commas.

---

1 **Look carefully at this piece of writing. Circle the mistakes that have been made with inverted commas, punctuation and capital letters.**

"Stop! Thief"! yelled the shopkeeper.

Max asked, "what's the matter?"

"That man stole the money from the till, replied the shopkeeper."

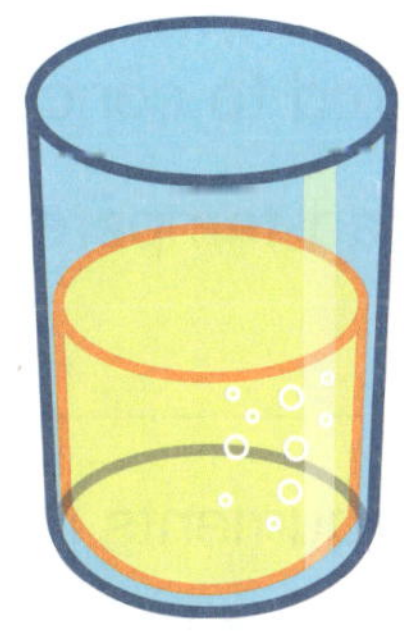

Max asked", Which way did he go?"

The shopkeeper said, "Over the bridge towards the station".

"I'll follow him, and you phone the police", shouted Max.

"You can't escape", panted Max as he ran after the thief.

'You'll never catch me!," replied the thief.

2 **Add inverted commas and punctuation to these sentences.**

a Wesley said We're going to Spain on holiday

b Can I have a drink please asked Lola

c Ouch yelled Kira

d Luke asked What time is it

e My big brother shouted Get out

Balanced arguments

A balanced argument needs to include both points of view.

Connectives like *if*, *also*, *then*, *although*, *however* and *on the other hand*, allow us to compare different points of view.

1   **Underline the connectives in this argument.**

> If you spend all your pocket money on sweets, then you will not have any left to buy other things. Also, sweets are bad for your teeth.
>
> On the other hand, if you save some of your pocket money you will be able to buy something you really want. Although it can take a while to save enough, it will be worth it in the end.

2   **Here is an argument about whether children should be allowed to choose when they go to bed. Pick connectives from the box to complete the argument.**

if   then   on the other hand   however   although   also

___________________ children know how tired they feel, they are too young to understand how much sleep they really need. ___________________ children are allowed to decide when they go to bed, ___________________ they may be too tired to concentrate at school. ___________________, tired children can be very bad-tempered, which could cause arguments at home.

___________________, being able to choose their own bedtimes may actually save arguments in the family. Children can always catch up with sleep at the weekends. ___________________, this would use up a lot of their free time.

Alliteration

Alliteration is when several words next to each other, or very close together, begin with the **same sound**.

one **wh**ite **w**ig

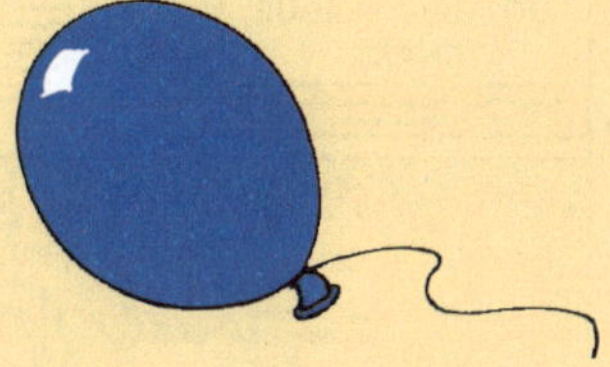

bright **bl**ue **b**alloon

Using alliteration draws attention to that part of your writing and helps to add rhythm, especially in poetry.

1 Underline the alliteration in each sentence.

a Daisy danced daintily across the stage.

b Crystal the cat crept cautiously to the door.

c Katie bought a pink patterned purse.

d Philip found frogs in the pond.

e Noble knights never run from battle.

f Gemma tells tall tales.

g Rachel's rabbits wriggled in her arms.

h Nasty gnomes never play fair.

2 Finish each phrase by adding two more words that start with the same sound.

a beautiful babies ___________________ ___________________

b tall trees ___________________ ___________________

c honest ogres ___________________ ___________________

d sleepy Simon ___________________ ___________________

e careful Cara ___________________ ___________________

f fat fairies ___________________ ___________________

g poor Peter ___________________ ___________________

h reckless rhinos ___________________ ___________________

The *g* sound spelt *gue* and the *k* sound spelt *que*

English has lots of French words and spellings as part of the language. These spellings can be tricky, so it is a pattern you just have to learn and remember.

league

mosque

1 Learn these spellings using the LOOK, COVER, WRITE, CHECK method.

a league _____________________ d plague _____________________

b tongue _____________________ e rogue _____________________

c fatigue _____________________

Write other words that use the pattern gue for the g sound.

____

2 Learn these spellings using the LOOK, COVER, WRITE, CHECK method. Write a sentence for each word to show you understand the meaning.

a antique ____

b unique ____

c mosque ____

d cheque ____

e opaque ____

Write other words that use the pattern que for the k sound.

____

Its and *it's*

Apostrophes are used to **shorten** and **join** words together.

It is my parrot ➡ **It's** my parrot

They also show when something belongs to someone.

Sian**'s** parrot.

These are called possessive apostrophes. The only exception is *it*, which never has a possessive apostrophe.

*The parrot flapped **its** wings.*

1 **Add the apostrophe to *its* in these sentences if it is necessary.**

a The cat licked its paws.

b Its my favourite book.

c Its starting to rain.

d The hamster escaped from its cage.

e In the autumn the tree loses its leaves.

f Its easier to roller-skate than ice-skate.

g The dog wagged its tail.

2 **Rewrite these sentences, replacing the words in bold with *its* or *it's*.**

a I like popcorn, because **it is** sweet and crunchy.

____

b **It is** important to take care when you cross the road.

____

c The bird flapped **the bird's** wings.

____

d **It is** hot today.

____

e When **the clock's** battery ran down, the clock stopped working.

____

f The flower opened **the flower's** petals.

____

Test 1 The suffix *ous*

Lots of words end in the suffix *ous*. Some words just add *ous* to the root word.

mountain

mountain**ous**

For some *ous* words, *our* in the root word changes to *or*.

vig**our** ➞ vig**or**ous

Add the suffix *ous* to these words. Write the new words.

1. poison________ ___________________________________

2. danger________ ___________________________________

3. mountain______ ___________________________________

4. courage_______ ___________________________________

5. outrage_______ ___________________________________

6. humour________ ___________________________________

7. glamour_______ ___________________________________

Add the suffix *ous* to complete these words.

8. fam____________

9. vari___________

10. tremend________

11. enorm__________

12. jeal___________

13. seri___________

14. obvi___________

15. curi___________

 Which suffix?

These suffixes sound the same.

tion

sion

ssion

cian

Use what you know about the suffixes *tion*, *sion*, *ssion* and *cian* to write the correct one to complete each word.

1. musi___________

2. se___________

3. complica___________

4. deci___________

5. mi___________

6. ver___________

7. electri___________

8. adop___________

9. expre___________

10. magi___________

11. addi___________

12. televi___________

13. conclu___________

14. physi___________

15. alloca___________

Colour in your score

Verb tenses

Verbs can be written in different **tenses**.

This happened in the **past**. The verb is in the **past tense**.

This is happening **now**. The verb is in the **present tense**.

This will happen in the **future**. The verb is in the **future tense**.

Write if the verb in bold is past, present or future tense.

1. I **will go** out to play after tea. __________

2. We **rode** our bikes. __________

3. I **am swimming** in the sea. __________

4. The girl **dropped** her bag in the mud. __________

5. Tomorrow I **will take** my ruler to school. __________

6. I **like** crisps. __________

7. My mum **gave** me some lunch. __________

8. In the summer I **will fly** on a plane. __________

9. I **sleep** in the top bunk. __________

10. My brother **snores**. __________

11. The car **crashed** into a wall. __________

12. Soon the ambulance **will arrive**. __________

13. Next week I **will leave** for Paris. __________

14. Last year I **went** to Spain. __________

15. I **drew** a picture in my book. __________

Colour in your score

15 14 13 12 11 10 9 8 7 6 5 4 3 2 1

Write some sentences of your own in the past, present & future tense.

34

Test 4 The *k* sound spelt *ch*

The *k* sound spelt *ch* comes from the ancient Greeks. This pattern can be tricky to remember, so it is something that just has to be practised. Build your own **dictionary** – it is always good to use new vocabulary.

Write the meaning of these words. If you do not know the words, look them up in the dictionary.

1. scheme _______________________________
2. chorus _______________________________
3. echo _______________________________
4. chemist _______________________________
5. character _______________________________
6. ache _______________________________
7. school _______________________________
8. chemistry _______________________________
9. chaos _______________________________
10. chameleon _______________________________
11. anchor _______________________________
12. archive _______________________________
13. architect _______________________________
14. chasm _______________________________
15. choir _______________________________

15
14
13
12
11
10
9
8
7
6
5
4
3
2
1

Colour in your score

Test 5 Suffixes *er* and *or*

A suffix is a **group of letters** we add to the **end of a word**.
A suffix changes the **meaning** of a word or the **job the word does**.

paint (verb)

paint**er** (noun)

Add either the suffix *er* or *or* to make these verbs into nouns. Take care with the spelling.

1. bake _______________________
2. visit _______________________
3. detect _______________________
4. clean _______________________
5. build _______________________
6. edit _______________________
7. calculate _______________________
8. dance _______________________
9. sail _______________________
10. print _______________________
11. radiate _______________________
12. swim _______________________
13. inspect _______________________
14. act _______________________
15. skate _______________________

Test 6 Alphabetical order

Many **reference books** are organised in alphabetical order.

These words are organised in alphabetical order according to the **third** letter.

These words are organised in alphabetical order according to the **fourth** letter.

Order these words according to their third letter.

1. acrobat   act   acorn   _______________________

2. bacon   baby   badge   _______________________

3. beach   between   bend   _______________________

4. daisy   dance   dam   _______________________

5. door   dock   doughnut   _______________________

6. fig   fire   film   _______________________

Order these words according to their fourth letter.

7. climb   cliff   clinic   _______________________

8. drink   drill   drift   _______________________

9. earth   early   earn   _______________________

10. margarine   marsh   market   _______________________

11. herring   herb   hero   _______________________

12. blanket   blast   black   _______________________

13. brown   brother   broccoli   _______________________

14. script   scrap   screen   _______________________

15. through   thrust   threw   _______________________

Test 7 Homophones

Homophones are words that **sound alike** but have **different spellings** and **meanings**.

I **heard** a **herd** of elephants coming towards me.

① **Write the correct word to complete each sentence.**

1. The _________ shone in the sky.   (sun/son)

2. I _________ my bike.   (rode/road)

3. He ate the _________ cake.   (hole/whole)

4. I had a _________ of pie.   (peace/piece)

5. I tied a _________ in the string.   (not/knot)

6. You have to _________ an apple.   (peal/peel)

7. I measured my _________.   (waste/waist)

8. The man took the quickest _________.   (route/root)

9. The _________ landed at the airport.   (plane/plain)

10. What _________ do you eat for breakfast?   (cereal/serial)

11. It is wrong to _________.   (steal/steel)

12. Bald men have no _________ on their heads.   (hairs/hares)

13. The ship had two _________.   (sales/sails)

14. The children took _________ bags.   (there/their)

15. It's easy to get _________.   (board/bored)

② Now pick 5 and add 2 or 3 new ideas to the sentence to build a complex sentence.

Colour in your score

Test 8 Soft *ch*

The soft *ch* sound that sounds like 'sh' usually means
the word has come from the French language and
has become part of the English language.

Write the meaning of these words. If you do not know the words, look them up in the dictionary.

1. chef ______________________________

2. chalet ______________________________

3. machine ______________________________

4. brochure ______________________________

5. chauffeur ______________________________

6. moustache ______________________________

7. parachute ______________________________

8. chaperone ______________________________

9. chandelier ______________________________

10. panache ______________________________

11. quiche ______________________________

12. crochet ______________________________

13. chiffon ______________________________

14. charade ______________________________

15. ricochet ______________________________

Colour in your score

Test 9 Sound spelt *sc*

Some spellings show the way the English language has developed over time. The soft *sc* sound comes from the Latin language – used by the ancient Romans.

Learn these spellings, then write a short sentence that contains each word to show you understand the meaning. You can use a dictionary to help you.

1. science   ______________________________

2. scene   ______________________________

3. discipline   ______________________________

4. fascinate   ______________________________

5. crescent   ______________________________

6. disciple   ______________________________

7. scenic   ______________________________

8. scientific   ______________________________

9. fascination   ______________________________

10. disciplined   ______________________________

11. scent   ______________________________

12. scythe   ______________________________

13. fascinator   ______________________________

14. scientist   ______________________________

15. scenery   ______________________________

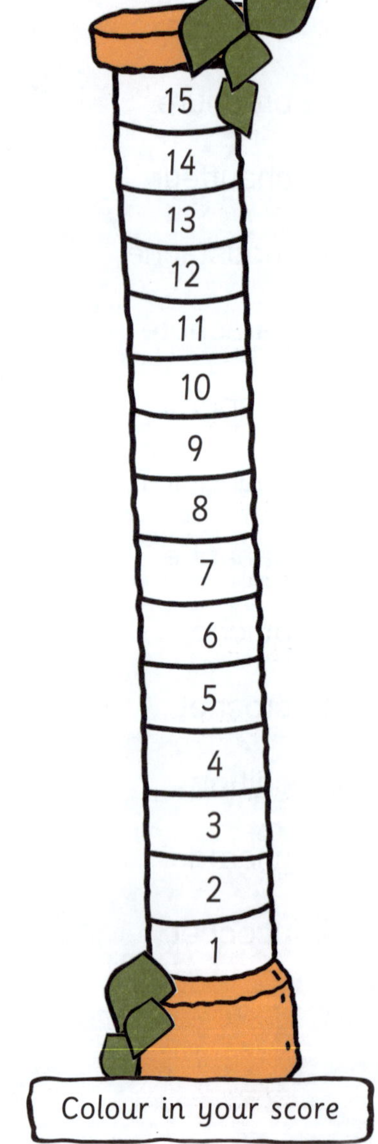

Test 10 Adverbs

quick – quick**ly**

We can just add *ly* to many adjectives to make adverbs.

merry – merr**ily**

If the word ends in *y*, we change the *y* to *i* and add *ly*.

miserable – miserab**ly**

If the word ends in *le*, we often drop the *le* and add *ly*.

Change these adjectives into adverbs ending in *ly*.

1. sweet _______________________
2. hungry _______________________
3. simple _______________________
4. plain _______________________
5. proud _______________________
6. noble _______________________
7. idle _______________________
8. glad _______________________
9. angry _______________________
10. feeble _______________________
11. easy _______________________
12. willing _______________________
13. lazy _______________________
14. possible _______________________
15. steady _______________________

Test 11 WOW words

WOW words make your writing more exciting.

Underline the most exciting and descriptive word in each pair.

1. cold   freezing

2. windy   blustery

3. hot   blistering

4. excruciating   painful

5. wet   drenched

6. parched   dry

7. dirty   filthy

8. old   ancient

9. glittering   shining

10. delighted   pleased

11. nice   wonderful

12. amazing   surprising

13. nasty   wicked

14. beautiful   gorgeous

15. massive   big

Test 12 Similes

A simile is when we **compare** one thing to another, using the words *as* or *like*.

1 Choose the best adjective to complete each simile.

heavy	black	red	quiet	playful	
	sweet	soft	green	smooth	wise
white	fierce	cool	light	slippery	

1. as _______ as honey

2. as _______ as a kitten

3. as _______ as silk

4. as _______ as butter

5. as _______ as a cucumber

6. as _______ as an owl

7. as _______ as beetroot

8. as _______ as a lion

9. as _______ as grass

10. as _______ as an eel

11. as _______ as snow

12. as _______ as lead

13. as _______ as a feather

14. as _______ as a mouse

15. as _______ as coal

2 Now write a paragraph and describe an animal in detail. Use some similes.

Colour in your score

Test 13 Handwriting

Neat handwriting is important because it makes
your work attractive and easier to read.

Write out these sentences using your best joined-up handwriting. Pay special attention to the spacing of your letters, and their size in relation to one another.

1. I went for a walk in the woods with my granny.

   ____

2. The sun made lovely patterns on the ground.

   ____

3. We saw a beautiful red squirrel in the trees.

   ____

4. Its tail puffed out behind it as it jumped.

   ____

5. There were lots of nuts under the tree.

   ____

6. They had holes gnawed in them by the squirrel.

   ____

7. I picked one up to take home.

   ____

8. I collect things in the woods for my nature table.

   ____

9. I collected red oak leaves and spiky conker cases.

   ____

10. I picked up some sycamore keys and maple seeds.

   ____

Colour in your score

Test 14 Words containing *y*

In some words, the soft *i* sound is spelt with a *y*.

**Underline the correctly spelt word in each pair.
Cross out the incorrect word.**

1. myth   mith
2. histerical   hysterical
3. mistery   mystery
4. cignet   cygnet
5. strict   stryct
6. cristal   crystal
7. pyramid   piramid
8. slypper   slipper
9. gim   gym
10. glisten   glysten
11. trist   tryst
12. pencil   pencyl
13. glympse   glimpse
14. rhithm   rhythm
15. plimsoll   plymsoll

Test 15 More suffixes

A suffix is a **group of letters** we add to the **end** of a word.

A suffix changes the **meaning** of the word or the **job the word does**.

Sometimes you need to change the spelling of the root word before you add the suffix.

*magic – magic**al***

Choose the correct suffix to complete each word.

1. music__________ (al/ous)

2. fashion__________ (able/ible)

3. merry__________ (ment/ous)

4. comic__________ (ment/al)

5. amuse__________ (ous/ment)

6. reverse__________ (able/ible)

7. employ__________ (ment/al)

8. inspect__________ (ion/ment)

9. forgot__________ (able/en)

10. arrange__________ (ion/ment)

11. intense__________ (ate/ive)

12. entertain__________ (ment/al)

13. relate__________ (ion/al)

14. season__________ (al/ise)

15. act__________ (ment/ion)

Test 16 Dictation

Dictation is really useful when you want to take notes so you can remember things.

1. I went out at night to look at the stars.

2. It was cold outside.

3. I wore a big jumper, a coat and a hat.

4. Mum gave me some gloves to wear.

5. I saw a bat fluttering around the garden.

6. It was chasing the moths flying round the light.

7. The moon was very bright.

8. It lit up the garden.

9. I saw the moon reflecting in the pond.

10. I looked at a star chart, and found some patterns.

11. I managed to find Orion's Belt.

12. Mum showed me the Great Bear.

13. It was getting very late.

14. We came inside and had toast for supper.

15. I'd had a lovely time!

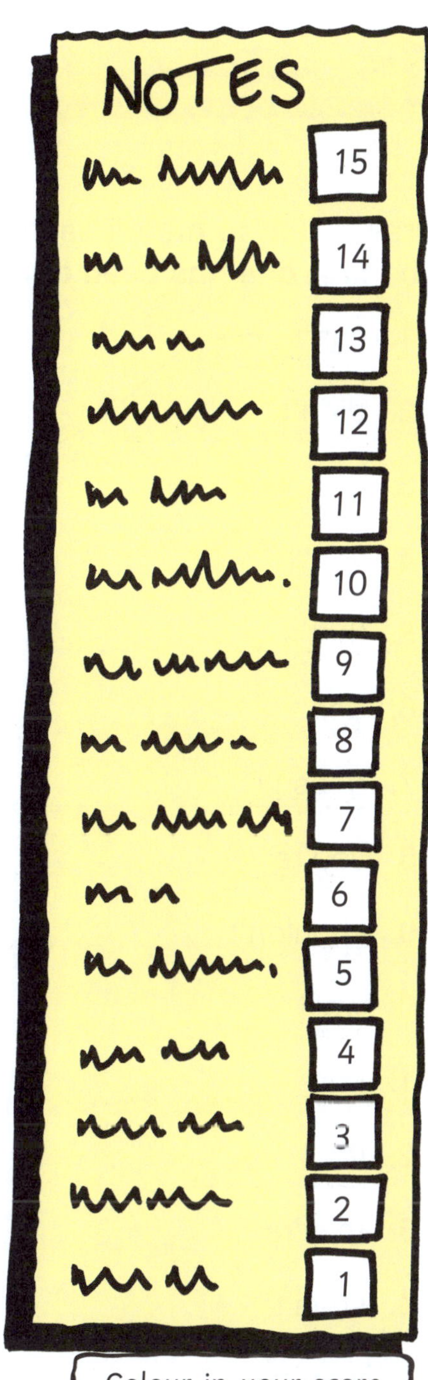

Test 17 Contractions

We sometimes **shorten** a word by **leaving out** some letters.
These shortened words are called contractions.
We use an **apostrophe** to show where letters have been left out.

Draw a line to match each contraction to its longer form.
The first one has been done for you.

1. can't		we have
2. didn't		do not
3. we've		can not
4. you'll		it is
5. that's		did not
6. don't		I would
7. doesn't		shall not
8. you're		does not
9. shouldn't		they are
10. we'll		you will
11. I'd		will not
12. it's		should not
13. they're		we will
14. shan't		that is
15. won't		you are

Commas

Long ago, dinosaurs roamed the earth.

Commas are used to separate **extra bits** that are **added** to sentences.

The car, a red one, was parked outside the shop.

Commas help to **break up** longer sentences **into smaller parts**.

Write the missing commas in each of these sentences. Then copy the sentence into your homework book.

1. That boy the smaller one shouted rude names at me.

2. Don't do that Sam!

3. Pass me my cup of tea please.

4. Feeling rather tired Goldilocks sat down on the chair.

5. Let's go out shall we?

6. Whenever I can I like to go out.

7. Pick up your bag Anna.

8. The dog a spotted Dalmatian escaped from the garden.

9. If I can find one I always buy a comic.

10. Quiet please!

11. No I don't want a sandwich.

12. Whether it's rugby or football I enjoy the game.

13. What's the matter Mrs Shah?

14. Once upon a time there lived an ugly troll.

15. That's very nice thank you.

Test 19 Word order

Sometimes when we **change the order** of words, it **changes the meaning** of the sentence.

The dog chased the postman.   The postman chased the dog.

① **Rewrite these sentences so they make sense.**

1. The sandwich ate a man. ______________________________
2. The car got into the prince. ______________________________
3. The crown put on his king. ______________________________
4. The laugh made us clown. ______________________________
5. The tree climbed the squirrel. ______________________________
6. The piano played the teacher. ______________________________
7. The trunk lifted its elephant. ______________________________
8. The ball kicked a footballer. ______________________________
9. Some boots wore children. ______________________________
10. The runway landed on the plane. ______________________________
11. An egg fried the girl. ______________________________
12. The bone picked up the dog. ______________________________
13. The television is watching Sam. ______________________________
14. A tunnel went through the train. ______________________________
15. Stripes have tigers. ______________________________

② Now pick 5 sentences & write a more complex sentence by adding extra ideas. Try to use a comma.

Colour in your score

50

Test 20 Apostrophes marking possession

We use an apostrophe to show **ownership** (that something belongs to someone).

When there is **only one** owner, we usually write 's.

When there is **more than one** owner, we usually write s'.

the boy**'s** books
(the books belong to one boy)

the boy**s'** books
(the books belong to more than one boy)

Write the shortened form of each phrase.

1. the bike belongs to the girl — *the girl's bike*

2. the pen belongs to the bo — _______________

3. the car belongs to the man — _______________

4. the cup belongs to my brother — _______________

5. the nuts belong to the squirrels — _______________

6. the ship belongs to the sailors — _______________

7. the school belongs to the teachers — _______________

8. the tie belongs to Sam — _______________

9. the bag belongs to Dr Smith — _______________

10. the cubs belong to the lion — _______________

11. the bananas belong to the monkeys — _______________

12. the ball belongs to the footballers — _______________

13. the guitar belongs to the singer — _______________

14. the barn belongs to the farmer — _______________

15. the hose belongs to the fire-fighters — _______________

Test 21 Comprehension (1)

Comprehension is a great way to check you have understood the things you have read.

Read this passage and answer the questions.

I like making models. I collect packaging and scraps, and make them into art! I use old newspaper and PVA glue to make papier-mâché.

My favourite models to make are dragons. I have made a family of different sizes and shapes, and have decorated them with beads, sequins and feathers. The wings are made by carefully cutting shapes from big plastic drinks bottles, and taping them to the bodies of the dragons. I have suspended my flock of dragons from my bedroom ceiling with clear thread, so it looks like they are flying.

1. What does the writer make models from?

   ____

2. What creatures does the writer like making best of all?

   ____

3. What decorations has the writer used?

   ____

4. What are the wings made from?

   ____

5. How does the writer hang her models from the ceiling?

   ____

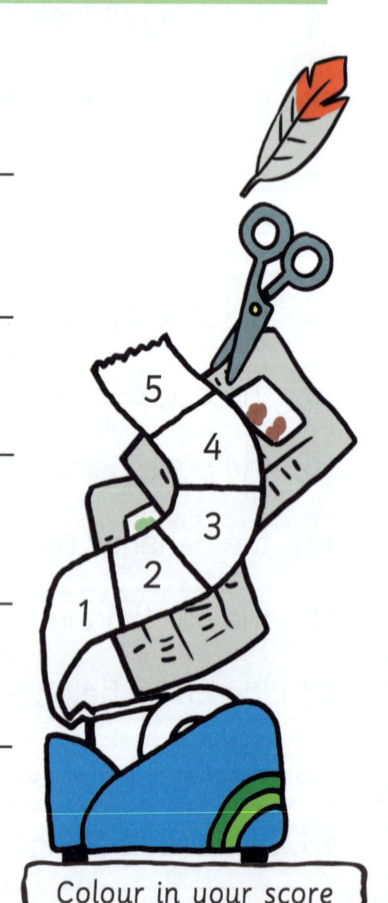

Colour in your score

Test 22 Comprehension (2)

Comprehension tests your reading skills and understanding.

Read this passage and answer the questions.

The hare ran across the moor, its long legs pumping up and down. Everything was starting to grow again, and everything smelled fresh. The hare stopped to sniff the air.

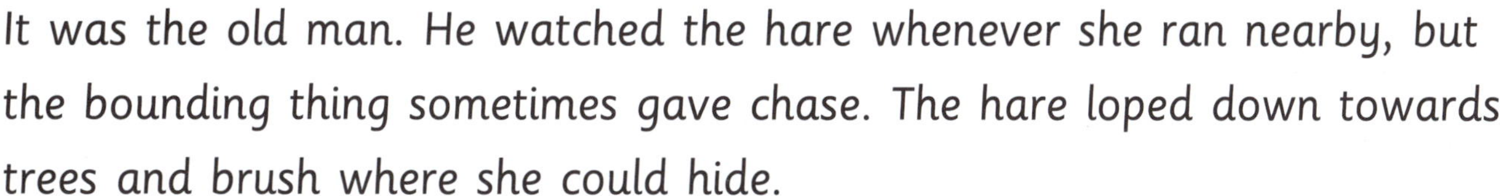

Down the hill, the hare saw two figures. One ran ahead, bounding and jumping. One walked slowly. It was the old man. He watched the hare whenever she ran nearby, but the bounding thing sometimes gave chase. The hare loped down towards trees and brush where she could hide.

The hare settled down cautiously, and the noise of the walkers faded. She dozed as the sun warmed her whiskers.

1. Where does the action of this story take place?

   ____

2. What does the hare see, down the hill?

   ____

3. What creature – 'the bounding thing' – do you think is with the old man?

   ____

4. Where did the hare hide?

   ____

5. Why do you think the hare is 'cautious'?

   ____

Colour in your score

Test 23 The word endings *ssion* and *cian*

The word endings *ssion* and *cian* **sound similar** so spelling these words can be tricky.

For root words ending in *ss* or *mit*, use the suffix *ssion*.

express ➡ expre**ssion**

For root words ending in *c* or *cs*, use the suffix *cian*.

electric ➡ electri**cian**

Add *ssion* or *cian* to complete each word.

1. magi__________

2. mi__________

3. musi__________

4. permi__________

5. politi__________

6. discu__________

7. confe__________

8. techni__________

9. beauti__________

10. aggre__________

11. commi__________

12. mathemati__________

13. profe__________

14. clini__________

15. impre__________

Test 24 Types of sentences

There are **four** different types of sentences.

A **question** asks something.

A **statement** gives information.

A **command** tells someone to do something.

An **exclamation** shows someone feels strongly about something.

Write what type of sentence each of these is.

1. The door is shut. ____________
2. Where is my bag? ____________
3. Go and have a bath. ____________
4. What a muddy T-shirt! ____________
5. When are you going? ____________
6. It's not fair! ____________
7. I'm going to bed. ____________
8. Turn off the television. ____________
9. I think that's wonderful! ____________
10. How did you get lost? ____________
11. Tom likes tennis. ____________
12. Cut the paper with scissors. ____________
13. Put the kettle on. ____________
14. Help! ____________
15. Who are you going with? ____________

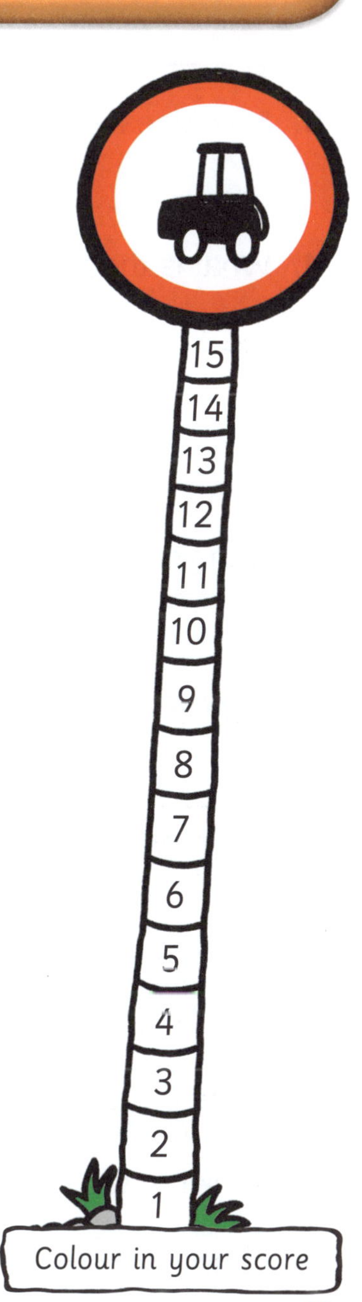

Test 25 Story writing (1) – planning

Plotting a story before you start
writing helps to keep your story
focused and moving forward.

Make notes to plot a story about a child moving to a new town.

1. Where is your story set?

2. Who are your cast of characters?

3. How does your story open? Make it exciting!

4. What is the main problem that needs to be overcome?

5. Who will overcome the problem, and how?

6. Can you identify the theme of your story?

7. How will you build up excitement or suspense?

8. Are there any unexpected events or plot twists?

9. How does the story end?

10. Can you think of a strong final sentence that will leave the reader
    thinking about your story long after they have finished reading?

56

Test 26 The word endings *tion* and *sion*

The two common word endings *tion* and *sion* sometimes get confused.

*invita**tion***

The *tion* at the end of
words sounds like 'shun'.

*televi**sion***

The *sion* at the end of
words sounds like 'zhon'.

**The ending of each of these words is wrong.
Write each word correctly.**

1. conversasion   ___________________________

2. explotion   ___________________________

3. sucsion   ___________________________

4. invation   ___________________________

5. confution   ___________________________

6. preparasion   ___________________________

7. creasion   ___________________________

8. revition   ___________________________

9. competision   ___________________________

10. populasion   ___________________________

11. divition   ___________________________

12. composision   ___________________________

13. conclution   ___________________________

14. inclution   ___________________________

15. fracsion   ___________________________

Test 27 The word endings *able* and *ible*

The two common word endings *able* and *ible* sometimes get confused.

comfort + able = comfortable

It is often possible to see the root word when *able* is added.

horror + ible = horrible

It is not always possible to see the root word when *ible* is added.

Choose *able* or *ible* to complete each word.

1. poss__________

2. reason__________

3. terr__________

4. reli__________

5. fashion__________

6. flex__________

7. remark__________

8. suit__________

9. respons__________

10. revers__________

11. sens__________

12. valu__________

13. miser__________

14. favour__________

15. vis__________

Test 28 Story writing (2) – characters

Great characters are so important for any story.
Characters are the things people often remember
when they think about books they have read.

Use these questions to build a strong 'hero' or protagonist for the story you planned in test 25.

1. Describe your character's physical appearance.

    ____

2. Describe their style of dress.

    ____

3. Is their hair unusually styled or coloured?

    ____

4. What is your character's face like?

    ____

5. How does your character's voice sound?

    ____

6. Does your character have any odd habits?

    ____

7. Does your character have a job?

    ____

8. Does your character have a car?

    ____

9. Does your character have a family or friends?

    ____

10. Does your character have a pet?

    ____

 Conjunctions

A conjunction is a **joining** word. It may be used to join two sentences.

The car was speeding. It passed the shop.

(two sentences)

The car was speeding **as** it passed the shop.

(one sentence with a conjunction)

Find and underline the conjunction in each sentence.

1. It rained heavily but we carried on with the game.

2. The teacher opened the door and the children came in.

3. I went to the shop but it was closed.

4. The children went outside and played in the garden.

5. The monkey will not come unless you give it a banana.

6. He was given the prize because he deserved it.

7. I got lost when I drove through the town.

8. I gave her another sweet as she had eaten the last one.

9. He bought me the present although he couldn't afford it.

10. Do not climb the tree or you might fall.

11. You will not pass the test if you don't try harder.

12. I went indoors when it began raining.

13. The girl will not go to school unless her mother brings her.

14. We started early so we would finish in time for tea.

15. I was nervous as I hadn't seen my uncle for a long time.

Now write some sentences using conjunctions.

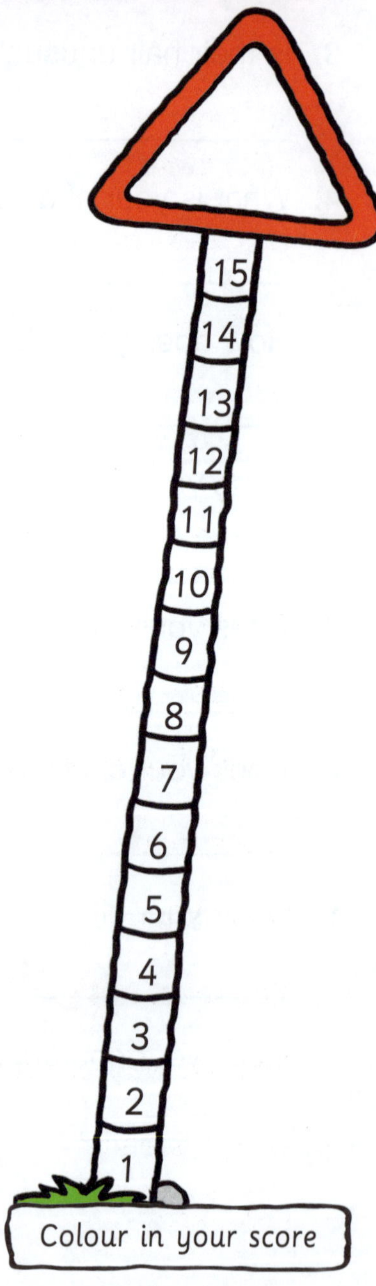

Test 30 Positive and negative

This is a **positive** sentence. It means "**yes**".

This is a **negative** sentence. It means "**no**".

The main negative is *not* or *n't*.

Write whether each sentence is positive or negative.

1. I like sweets. ______________

2. Lee was not a good boy. ______________

3. It did not stop raining. ______________

4. Ben won the race. ______________

5. I didn't do my homework last night. ______________

6. You should always smile. ______________

7. You should never tell lies. ______________

8. My drawing is nice. ______________

9. I don't like spelling. ______________

10. I hate maths. ______________

11. Don't shout. ______________

12. You must not run. ______________

13. The old lady could not lift the box. ______________

14. I can't whistle. ______________

15. I can knit. ______________

ANSWERS

Page 2

1. Make sure your child can ask questions about schools in the past, and listen carefully to the answers. Encourage your child to think about a variety of topics such as school subjects, food, playtimes and friends.

2. Make sure your child can write an account of the interview that looks at similarities and differences between schools in the past, when the interviewee was at school, and the present day.

Page 3

1. a new
   b whole
   c great
   d their
   e too or to
   f heard
   g see
   h bee
   i four or fore
   j right or rite

2. Any sentences that show your child understands the words given.

Page 4

1. a jumping
   b preferred
   c kicks
   d grabbed
   e gardening
   f saved, saving
   g lifts, lifting

2. a stopped
   b limited
   c carried
   d washes
   e began
   f explores

Page 5

1. a merriment
   b kindness
   c fitness
   d enjoyment
   e laziness
   f membership
   g silliness
   h friendship
   i carelessness
   j happiness

2. a measurement
   b tidiness
   c nastiness
   d employment
   e statement
   f wickedness
   g fellowship
   h apprenticeship
   i replacement
   j championship

Page 6

1. Chat with your child about their favourite film. Make sure they understand the questions, and how much detail to give in their answers.
   a Title of a favourite film.
   b Explanation of why the favourite character is a favourite.
   c An opinion, backed up with reasons, about the most exciting part of the film.
   d An opinion given about the ending, with mention of any problems that have been resolved.

2. a Any 'day out' place mentioned and reason for going (i.e. 'to see the waterfall'; 'to look at sculptures').
   b Description of the journey.
   c Description of the events of the day.
   d Opinion about whether the child would like to repeat the day out.
   e Opinion on whether the day out was good enough to be recommended to a friend.

Page 7

1. a submarine
   b success
   c sudden
   d sugar
   e suitable
   f summer
   g sunny
   h super
   i suspect

2. a hail
   b hair
   c hard
   d hare
   e harp
   f haste
   g hat
   h have

Page 8

1. a completely
   b comically
   c usually
   d sleepily
   e badly
   f totally
   g humbly
   h basically
   i gently

2. Any suitable adverb that makes a sensible sentence.

Page 9

1. a deepen
   b shorten
   c standardise
   d apologise
   e notify
   f elasticate
   g purify
   h formalise
   i waken
   j medicate

2. a intensify
   b realise
   c strengthen
   d simplify
   e harden
   f glorify
   g hasten
   h classify
   i serialise
   j weaken

Page 10

1. a hurt
   b put
   c ran
   d brought
   e sent
   f fell

2. a Yesterday, I ate my birthday cake.
   b Last week, Jamilla bought a comic.
   c Earlier today, Ali drew a picture.
   d Last night, I was tired.
   e When I was four, I could swim.
   f Yesterday, I told you a secret.

Page 11

1. a After tea, we played football.
   b Find your trainers, Paul.
   c Suddenly, the lights went out.
   d Judy and James, from next door, came shopping with us.
   e My hat, which is black, matches my scarf.
   f Last Tuesday, after school, I went skating.

2. a Tomorrow, we are playing football.
   b The ink, which was blue, stained the carpet.
   c Eventually, Jane won the game.
   d It's time to go, Ali.
   e While we were on holiday, we stayed in a hotel.
   f At school, in my classroom, is a display about trains.

Page 12

1. a hobbles b argues c devours
   shuffles   dictates   munches
   ambles   declares   chews
   Accept any additional verbs that are suitable.

2. The powerful verbs should appear in the following order in the story: ordered, yelled, shot, clambered, crept, gazed, grabbed, fled, hacked, crashed

Page 13

1. a she ate her breakfast.
   b he waited for his lunch.
   c he watched the stars.
   d I'll make lots of festive cakes and biscuits.
   e the hedgehog slept.
   f he packed his bags.
   g she watched out of the window.

2. Any sensible fronted adverbial followed by a comma.

Page 14

1. a while
   b before
   c after
   d soon
   e during

2. Any sentences which contain the adverb, conjunction or preposition given, and make sense.

Page 15

1. a sniffs
   b halves
   c puffs
   d cliffs
   e scarves
   f scuffs
   g calves
   h thieves
   i yourselves
   j knives

2. a loaves
   b selves
   c sheriffs
   d cuffs
   e wolves
   f wives
   g bluffs
   h shelves
   i elves
   j scoffs

Page 16

1. a starving
   b exhausted
   c lovely
   d horrible
   e terrifying
   f parched
   g drenched
   h hilarious

2. Many answers are possible. Any sensible choice of exciting words for each sentence

Page 17
1. Any more exciting, expanded sentence for each question in the style of the example.
2. Any interesting, descriptive sentences using each of the nouns given.

Page 18
1. a shocking f acidic
   b washable g roadworthy
   c trustworthy h amusing
   d beautiful i breakable
   e reliable j painful

2. a wishful f careful
   b agreeable g adorable
   c enviable h helpful
   d hopeful i valuable
   e wonderful j merciful

Page 19
1. Comparative adjectives are:
   b, d, f, g
   Superlative adjectives are:
   a, c, e, h

2. a tallest e oldest
   b narrower f more delicious
   c most amazing g strangest
   d better h less interesting

Page 20
1. The incorrect forms are:
   a Its' e wo'nt
   b hes f would'nt
   c did'nt g Your're
   d wel'l h Theyve

2. a mustn't d can't
   b you've e couldn't
   c shouldn't

Page 21
1. a the woman's bag
   b the boys' heads
   c the child's toy
   d the people's books
   e two dogs' baskets
   f the sun's rays
   g three footballers' boots
   h a cat's tail

2. a a bird's wings
   b the boys' pens
   c Kim's cat
   d Sam's parcels
   e my parents' car
   f the babies' rattles
   g my dad's wallet
   h the children's sweets

Page 22
1. a gratefully
   b conversationally
   c energetically
   d photographically
   e thankfully
   f joyfully
   g horrifically
   h respectfully

2. a correction, correctly
   b productive, production
   c constructive, construction
   d extremely, extremist
   e active, action
   f really, realist
   g oppressive, oppression
   h missive, mission

Page 23
1. a rhyming couplets
   b no rhyme
   c alternate rhyming lines

2. Any suitable poem endings that use the correct rhyming pattern

Page 24
1. Key words are likely to be:
   a <u>Molly</u> and <u>Sam</u> are <u>coming to tea</u>.
   b I have <u>gone for lunch</u>, but I will be <u>back at noon</u>.
   c <u>My birthday</u> is in <u>December</u>.
   d <u>Remember</u> you are playing <u>football</u> on <u>Saturday</u>.
   e I have <u>Maths</u> and <u>English homework</u> to do.
   f We need to <u>buy</u> some <u>milk</u> and <u>bread</u>.

2. Exact wording may vary.
   a Your tea is in the oven.
   b Brownies is at 6pm at the Town Hall.
   c Buy a gift for Lucy's party on Friday.
   d We are in the garden, come round the back of the house.
   e Your mum rang to say she is running late.
   f The car is fixed, so please come and collect it.

Page 25
1. a existing between nations
   b make again
   c car
   d underwater boat
   e remedy or medicine
   f play again, repeat
   g above/higher/better

2. a replace or reveal
   b substandard
   c interval
   d reveal or replace
   e antibiotics
   f supervise
   g automobile

Page 26
1. a The cat likes milk. She/He/It drinks it regularly.
   b Birds fly into our garden. They like our pond.
   c A man walked along the beach. He picked up shells.
   d The women were running. They were keeping fit.

2. Any sentences which contain a noun and a pronoun, and make sense.

Page 27
1. "Stop! Thief!" yelled the shopkeeper.
   Max asked, "What's the matter?"
   "That man stole the money from the till," replied the shopkeeper.
   Max asked, "Which way did he go?"
   The shopkeeper said, "Over the bridge towards the station."
   "I'll follow him, and you phone the police," shouted Max.
   "You can't escape," panted Max as he ran after the thief.
   "You'll never catch me," replied the thief.

2. a Wesley said, "We're going to Spain on holiday."
   b "Can I have a drink please?" asked Lola.
   c "Ouch!" yelled Kira.
   d Luke asked, "What time is it?"
   e My big brother shouted, "Get out!"

Page 28
1. <u>If</u> you spend all your pocket money on sweets, <u>then</u> you will not have any left to buy other things. <u>Also</u>, sweets are bad for your teeth. <u>On the other hand</u>, <u>if</u> you save some of your pocket money you will be able to buy something you really want. <u>Although</u> it can take a while to save enough, it will be worth it in the end.

2. Connectives should appear in this order: Although, If, then, Also, On the other hand, However

Page 29
1. a <u>Daisy danced daintily</u> across the stage.
   b <u>Crystal the cat crept cautiously</u> to the door.
   c Katie bought a <u>pink patterned purse</u>.
   d <u>Philip found frogs</u> in the pond.
   e <u>Noble knights never</u> run from battle.
   f Gemma <u>tells tall tales</u>.
   g <u>Rachel's rabbits wriggled</u> in her arms.
   h <u>Nasty gnomes never</u> play fair.

2. Any sensible answers that add words that start with the same sound.

Page 30
1. Can your child spell the words from memory? Any examples of *g* words spelt *gue*.

2. Can your child spell the words from memory? Any sentences which show understanding of the words given and any examples of *k* words spelt *que*.

ANSWERS

Page 31
1. The following sentences need an apostrophe:
   - **b** It's my favourite book.
   - **c** It's starting to rain.
   - **f** It's easier to roller-skate than ice-skate.

2. **a** I like popcorn, because it's sweet and crunchy.
   b It's important to take care when you cross the road.
   c The bird flapped its wings.
   d It's hot today.
   e When its battery ran down, the clock stopped working.
   f The flower opened its petals.

Page 32
1. poisonous
2. dangerous
3. mountainous
4. courageous
5. outrageous
6. humorous
7. glamorous
8. famous
9. various
10. tremendous
11. enormous
12. jealous
13. serious
14. obvious
15. curious

Page 33
The correct suffix is in **bold**.
1. musi**cian**
2. se**ssion**
3. complica**tion**
4. deci**sion**
5. mi**ssion**
6. ver**sion**
7. electri**cian**
8. adop**tion**
9. expre**ssion**
10. magi**cian**
11. addi**tion**
12. televi**sion**
13. conclu**sion**
14. physi**cian**
15. alloca**tion**

Page 34
1. future
2. past
3. present
4. past
5. future
6. present
7. past
8. future
9. present
10. present
11. past
12. future
13. future
14. past
15. past

Page 35
Any definitions which show understanding of the words given, for example:
1. plan, arrangement
2. part of a song repeated after each verse; a group of singers
3. a sound reflected back from a surface to the listener
4. person who carries out chemical research; a shop where medicines are supplied
5. person in a fictional piece of writing; the attributes of a person
6. throbbing pain
7. place where people learn
8. the science of 'matter' – what things are made up of
9. disorder, confusion
10. type of lizard
11. a weight used to hold a ship in place
12. collection of historical documents
13. person who designs buildings
14. deep opening in the earth's surface
15. group of singers

Page 36
1. baker
2. visitor
3. detector
4. cleaner
5. builder
6. editor
7. calculator
8. dancer
9. sailor
10. printer
11. radiator
12. swimmer
13. inspector
14. actor
15. skater

Page 37
1. acorn acrobat act
2. baby bacon badge
3. beach bend between
4. daisy dam dance
5. dock door doughnut
6. fig film fire
7. cliff climb clinic
8. drift drill drink
9. early earn earth
10. margarine market marsh
11. herb hero herring
12. black blanket blast
13. broccoli brother brown
14. scrap screen script
15. threw through thrust

Page 38
1. sun
2. rode
3. whole
4. piece
5. knot
6. peel
7. waist
8. route
9. plane
10. cereal
11. steal
12. hairs
13. sails
14. their
15. bored

Page 39
Any definitions which show understanding of the words given, for example:
1. person who cooks
2. wooden holiday home
3. piece of equipment that makes things
4. booklet with product information
5. a paid driver
6. strip of hair that grows above the lip
7. soft fabric cloth that helps things (including people) fall slowly (e.g. from a plane)
8. person who accompanies someone or a group of people, to keep them safe
9. large light fitting, usually containing crystals
10. flamboyant manner
11. savoury tart made with eggs
12. handicraft using wool and a hooked needle to make things such as blankets
13. type of sheer fabric
14. pretending; a game where words or phrases are acted out
15. something that rebounds off a surface

Page 40
Can your child spell the words from memory? Any sentences which show understanding of the words given.

Page 41
1. sweetly
2. hungrily
3. simply
4. plainly
5. proudly
6. nobly
7. idly
8. gladly
9. angrily
10. feebly
11. easily
12. willingly
13. lazily
14. possibly
15. steadily

Page 42
These words should be underlined.
1. freezing
2. blustery
3. blistering
4. excruciating
5. drenched
6. parched
7. filthy
8. ancient
9. glittering
10. delighted
11. wonderful
12. amazing
13. wicked
14. gorgeous
15. massive

Page 43
1. sweet
2. playful
3. smooth
4. soft
5. cool
6. wise
7. red
8. fierce
9. green
10. slippery
11. white
12. heavy
13. light
14. quiet
15. black